INVISIBLE INFLUENCE

Mastering Faceless Marketing
for Online Success

Henry Starks

HENRY STARKS
TRANSFORM YOUR LIFESTYLE

CONTENTS

INTRODUCTION

Dive into the realm of faceless marketing, where invisibility is your greatest asset. This guide unveils the power of operating behind the scenes, using advanced digital tools and strategies to influence markets and build brands without ever stepping into the spotlight.

INVISIBLE INFLUENCE:

*Mastering Faceless Marketing
for Online Success*

CHAPTER 1:
INTRODUCTION TO
INVISIBLE INFLUENCE

Defining Faceless Marketing

Faceless marketing represents a paradigm shift in the approach to online business and brand promotion, allowing individuals to thrive without the necessity of a personal brand or public visibility. This strategy emphasizes the use of innovative digital tools and techniques that enable creators, marketers, and entrepreneurs to build and promote their ventures while remaining behind the curtain. By leveraging various online platforms and technologies, faceless marketing empowers individuals to cultivate a successful presence in the digital marketplace without the traditional demands of personal exposure.

At the core of faceless marketing is the concept of anonymity, which can be a powerful asset for those who prefer to operate out of the public eye. Anonymous influencer campaigns exemplify this strategy, where brands collaborate with influencers who maintain a level of secrecy about their identities. These campaigns can create a sense of intrigue and authenticity, often resonating with audiences who value privacy and discretion. As a result, businesses can effectively reach targeted demographics without the pressure of personal branding, allowing for more focused and strategic marketing efforts.

AI-driven content creation is another crucial component of faceless marketing. By utilizing advanced algorithms and machine learning, marketers can generate high-quality content that engages audiences while minimizing the need for personal input. This technology enables creators to produce articles, videos, and graphics that align with their brand's message and goals. Additionally, voiceover marketing techniques allow for the delivery of information in a professional manner without revealing the creator's identity. This approach not only maintains anonymity but also ensures that the focus remains on the content itself rather than the creator.

Automated social media management tools further enhance the effectiveness of faceless marketing strategies. These platforms allow individuals to schedule, post, and analyze content across various channels without the constant personal engagement that traditional marketing demands. Privacy-focused ad strategies also play a significant role in this approach, enabling marketers to reach potential customers without compromising their personal information. By focusing on data-driven customer persona development, businesses can create targeted campaigns that resonate with their audience's interests and behaviors, all while maintaining the creator's anonymity.

In addition to these techniques, the utilization of stock footage and imagery, user-generated content curation, and virtual events can enrich the faceless marketing experience. By incorporating diverse elements such as visual storytelling and community engagement, brands can foster a strong connection with their audience without revealing the identities of the individuals behind the scenes. This multifaceted approach not only enhances brand visibility but also cultivates a sense of community and trust, which are essential for long-term success in the online business landscape. Through the principles of faceless marketing, individuals can achieve significant online success while preserving their privacy and personal boundaries.

THE RISE OF ANONYMOUS INFLUENCER CAMPAIGNS

The rise of anonymous influencer campaigns marks a significant shift in the landscape of online marketing, particularly for those who seek to establish a presence without the burden of personal branding. In an era where authenticity is often championed, the ability to remain faceless while effectively influencing consumer behavior presents a unique opportunity for individuals and creators. These campaigns leverage the power of anonymity to create compelling narratives and engage audiences without the need for a personal connection. This allows marketers to focus on the quality of content and the strategic deployment of messaging, rather than the persona behind it.

At the core of anonymous influencer campaigns is the utilization of AI-driven content creation. Advanced algorithms can analyze trends, audience preferences, and engagement metrics to generate content that resonates with target demographics. By harnessing AI technology, marketers can produce high-quality visuals, videos, and written materials that maintain consistency and appeal, all while remaining detached from a personal brand. This approach not only saves time but also allows for a broader reach, as the content can be tailored to various platforms and formats without the constraints associated with a single influencer's style.

Voiceover marketing techniques serve as another critical component in the rise of faceless campaigns. By employing professional voice actors or AI-generated voices, brands can convey messages with authority and emotional resonance without revealing the identity of the spokesperson. This method creates a layer of intrigue and can enhance the perceived credibility of the campaign. Furthermore, the use of voiceovers allows for diverse and dynamic storytelling, enabling brands to communicate complex ideas in an accessible manner while maintaining the anonymity of the creators behind the scenes.

Automated social media management tools have also played a pivotal role in facilitating anonymous influencer campaigns. These platforms enable businesses to schedule posts, analyze engagement data, and adjust strategies in real-time, all without the creator needing to be visibly present. This automation not only streamlines operations but also allows for the cultivation of a consistent online presence. Privacy-focused ad strategies can be seamlessly integrated into these campaigns, ensuring that brands adhere to ethical standards while effectively targeting their desired audience.

The curation of user-generated content further enhances the effectiveness of anonymous influencer campaigns. By encouraging customers to share their experiences and insights, brands can build a community-driven narrative that resonates with potential buyers. This strategy not only fosters authenticity but also positions the brand as a facilitator of conversation rather than a traditional marketer. Coupled with virtual brand ambassadors and the strategic use of stock footage and imagery, these tactics create a robust marketing framework that thrives without the need for individual visibility, allowing creators to succeed in the digital marketplace while maintaining their desired level of anonymity.

WHY PRIVACY MATTERS IN ONLINE BUSINESS

In an era where digital interactions dominate, understanding the importance of privacy in online business is paramount for those who prefer a faceless approach. Privacy not only safeguards personal information but also builds trust with consumers who are increasingly wary of how their data is used. For individuals and creators operating behind the scenes, maintaining privacy can enhance credibility and foster a reliable reputation. This trust is essential, as it encourages customers to engage with brands that respect their data and prioritize ethical practices.

The landscape of online marketing is evolving, and privacy regulations are becoming more stringent. Compliance with these regulations is crucial for businesses that want to avoid legal repercussions and maintain a positive public image. By adopting privacy-focused ad strategies, businesses can navigate these complexities while still effectively reaching their target audience. Utilizing anonymized data can help in developing customer personas without compromising individual privacy, allowing businesses to tailor their marketing efforts to meet specific needs without risking their integrity.

Moreover, the rise of AI-driven content creation and automated social media management presents unique opportunities for maintaining privacy while maximizing efficiency. These tools can generate and distribute content without revealing the identity of the creator, allowing for a seamless marketing experience. By leveraging technology, businesses can focus on producing high-quality content and engaging with their audience without the pressure of personal exposure. This approach not only enhances operational efficiency but also aligns with the privacy values that many consumers prioritize.

For those utilizing virtual brand ambassadors and voiceover marketing techniques, privacy serves as a protective barrier against potential backlash. Anonymity allows creators to explore diverse marketing strategies without the fear of personal judgment or negative publicity. This freedom can lead to more innovative and daring campaigns, fostering a unique connection with audiences that is based on content rather than personal identity. By prioritizing privacy, businesses can cultivate an environment of creativity and risk-taking that ultimately drives success.

In conclusion, the significance of privacy in online business cannot be overstated, especially for those seeking to thrive in a faceless manner. By embracing privacy-centric practices, businesses can enhance consumer trust, navigate regulatory landscapes, and leverage technology in ways that promote efficiency and innovation. In a world where consumers are increasingly protective of their data, prioritizing privacy is not just a strategic advantage; it is a foundational element for sustainable success in the online marketplace.

CHAPTER 2: UNDERSTANDING FACELESS MARKETING

The Concept of Faceless Branding

The concept of faceless branding revolutionizes the traditional approach to marketing by allowing individuals and businesses to establish a presence without the need for personal visibility. In a digital landscape where personal branding often dominates, faceless branding offers a compelling alternative. It empowers creators and entrepreneurs who prefer to remain behind the scenes, focusing on the quality of their offerings rather than their personal image. This allows for a unique positioning in the marketplace, where the brand itself becomes the focal point, rather than the individual behind it.

Faceless branding is particularly effective in the realm of anonymous influencer campaigns. These campaigns leverage the power of influencers who operate without revealing their identities, creating an intriguing mystique that can engage audiences on a different level. This anonymity fosters curiosity and allows brands to connect with consumers without the biases often associated with personal brands. As a result, brands can cultivate a diverse audience, appealing to various demographics while avoiding the pitfalls of individual representation.

Incorporating AI-driven content creation into faceless branding strategies enhances the overall efficiency and effectiveness of marketing efforts. By utilizing artificial intelligence to generate content, businesses can produce high-quality materials at scale while maintaining a consistent brand voice. This technology allows for the creation of engaging visuals, written content, and even video presentations without the need for direct involvement from individuals. As a result, businesses can focus on refining their brand message and strategy, leaving the content generation to sophisticated algorithms.

Voiceover marketing techniques play a crucial role in establishing a faceless brand identity. By employing professional voiceover artists, businesses can convey their messages effectively while maintaining anonymity. This strategy is particularly relevant in video content, where the voiceover can drive engagement without requiring the presence of a visible personality. The use of voiceovers can humanize a brand while allowing creators to remain behind the scenes, ensuring that the brand's essence is communicated without personal exposure.

Faceless branding also aligns seamlessly with privacy-focused ad strategies. In a world increasingly concerned with data privacy, consumers are drawn to brands that respect their anonymity. By focusing on creating value-driven content and employing user-generated content curation, businesses can engage customers without overwhelming them with personal marketing tactics. Virtual brand ambassadors and automated social media management further enhance this approach, enabling brands to maintain a consistent online presence while respecting consumer privacy. This strategy not only builds trust but also fosters a sense of community among users who feel safe engaging with brands that prioritize their anonymity.

BENEFITS OF REMAINING ANONYMOUS

Remaining anonymous in the digital marketplace offers a plethora of advantages that can significantly enhance the potential for success without the burden of personal visibility. For individuals and creators who prefer to operate behind the scenes, anonymity allows for a focus on the product rather than the persona. This approach can cultivate a more authentic connection with audiences who are drawn to the value of the content rather than the creator's identity. It establishes a unique environment where the emphasis is placed on delivering quality offerings, thereby enhancing engagement and fostering loyalty.

One of the primary benefits of maintaining anonymity is the freedom it provides in experimentation and creativity. Without the constraints of a personal brand, creators can explore various niches and marketing strategies without the fear of tarnishing their reputation. This flexibility encourages innovation and the ability to pivot quickly in response to market trends or audience preferences. By leveraging techniques such as AI-driven content creation, creators can produce high-quality materials that resonate with their target demographics while remaining faceless, allowing them to maintain a distinct separation from their public persona.

Anonymity also serves as a protective barrier against potential backlash or criticism. In an era where opinions can spread rapidly across social media, operating without a personal brand allows creators to avoid the emotional toll that can accompany public scrutiny. This shield can enhance mental well-being and provide the space necessary for consistent productivity. Furthermore, privacy-focused advertising strategies can be deployed without the risk of personal reputations being impacted, ensuring that marketing efforts remain effective and targeted.

Incorporating virtual brand ambassadors and automated social media management tools allows anonymous creators to maintain a strong online presence while preserving their privacy. These strategies enable consistent engagement with audiences through curated content and user-generated interactions, all managed behind the curtain of anonymity. Such tactics not only streamline operations but also establish a recognizable brand identity that thrives independently of the individual behind it.

Lastly, remaining anonymous can facilitate a data-driven approach to customer persona development. By focusing on analytics and audience insights rather than personal branding, creators can refine their strategies based on empirical evidence rather than subjective perceptions. This objective approach leads to more effective marketing campaigns, ensuring that the content resonates with audiences and drives conversions. As the landscape of faceless marketing continues to evolve, the benefits of anonymity remain a compelling aspect for those seeking to build successful online businesses without the need for direct visibility.

CASE STUDIES OF SUCCESSFUL FACELESS MARKETING

Case studies of successful faceless marketing provide valuable insights into how anonymity can be leveraged for impactful online business strategies. One notable example is an anonymous influencer campaign that successfully utilized a well-crafted narrative to engage an audience without revealing the identity of the creator. This approach allowed the brand to build a community based on shared values and interests rather than personal fame. By focusing on content that resonated deeply with the target demographic, this campaign achieved significant engagement rates and sales conversions, demonstrating the potential of faceless marketing strategies.

Another compelling case involves a company that effectively employed AI-driven content creation tools to produce high-quality video content without any on-camera presence. By utilizing advanced algorithms, the brand was able to generate tailored messaging that appealed to specific customer personas. The integration of voiceover marketing techniques enhanced the emotional connection with viewers, providing a polished and professional exterior without the need for a visible spokesperson. This method not only streamlined content production but also allowed for rapid scalability in response to market trends.

Virtual brand ambassadors have also emerged as a powerful tool in the realm of faceless marketing. A tech startup successfully implemented a virtual avatar to represent their brand across various online platforms. This avatar engaged with users through automated social media management, responding to inquiries and sharing relevant content. By maintaining a consistent online presence while ensuring anonymity, the brand could cultivate a loyal following and drive significant traffic to its website. This innovative approach showcases how digital personas can effectively fulfill roles traditionally held by human influencers.

The use of stock footage and imagery has proven to be another effective strategy in faceless marketing. A travel-related business capitalized on this by curating a library of high-quality stock visuals that aligned with their brand aesthetic. By creating visually compelling content that told a story without needing a personal touch, they were able to attract users and encourage user-generated content curation. This not only increased brand visibility but also fostered a community of users who contributed their own experiences, further amplifying the brand's reach while maintaining the faceless approach.

Lastly, privacy-focused ad strategies have gained traction in faceless marketing, particularly in the context of virtual events and webinars. A wellness brand successfully organized a series of webinars featuring industry experts while keeping the hosts' identities anonymous. By concentrating on the value of the content rather than the credentials of the speakers, the brand attracted a diverse audience interested in personal development. Data-driven customer persona development enabled the brand to tailor the content to specific needs, resulting in high attendance rates and increased brand loyalty. This case exemplifies how faceless marketing can thrive through thoughtful content curation and strategic audience engagement.

CHAPTER 3: ANONYMOUS INFLUENCER CAMPAIGNS

Identifying the Right Influencers

Identifying the right influencers is a critical step for individuals looking to build successful online businesses while maintaining a low profile. In the realm of faceless marketing, the selection of influencers who align with your brand ethos can significantly impact your campaign's effectiveness. It is essential to understand not only the influencers' reach but also their engagement rates, audience demographics, and content style. An influencer with a modest following but high engagement might be more beneficial than a larger influencer with a less engaged audience. This approach ensures that the selected influencer can genuinely resonate with the target market and drive authentic interactions.

When searching for suitable influencers, leveraging data-driven insights is indispensable. Utilizing analytics tools can help pinpoint influencers whose follower demographics closely match your target customer personas. This involves examining factors such as age, location, interests, and online behavior. By understanding these metrics, you can establish a more targeted approach to your influencer partnerships, ensuring that your message is delivered to the right audience. Additionally, consider the influencers' content themes and values to ensure alignment with your brand's mission, which is crucial for maintaining authenticity in your marketing efforts.

Another important aspect of identifying the right influencers is assessing their previous collaborations. Review their past campaigns to gauge how they interact with brands and how their audience responds. This analysis can provide insights into their ability to create engaging content that drives conversions. Pay attention to the style of content produced, as it should complement your own marketing strategies, whether that involves AI-driven content creation, user-generated content curation, or voiceover marketing techniques. The influencer's previous success with similar campaigns can serve as a strong indicator of their potential effectiveness for your brand.

In the context of virtual brand ambassadors and automated social media management, it is also crucial to consider the influencer's adaptability to various formats. Influencers who are skilled in creating diverse content—be it videos, stories, or posts —can enhance the versatility of your marketing strategy. This flexibility is particularly beneficial when planning for virtual events and webinars or when utilizing stock footage and imagery. An influencer who can seamlessly transition between different content types will be better equipped to engage audiences across multiple platforms.

Finally, privacy-focused ad strategies should guide your influencer selection process. As consumers become increasingly concerned about their online privacy, working with influencers who prioritize transparency and ethical marketing practices can enhance your brand's credibility. Influencers who openly share their partnership details with followers foster trust and encourage genuine engagement. By prioritizing these elements, you can cultivate a network of influencers who not only amplify your message but also align with your commitment to privacy and authenticity in marketing, ultimately driving sustainable growth for your online business.

COLLABORATING WITHOUT VISIBILITY

Collaborating without visibility offers a unique opportunity for individuals and creators seeking to build successful online businesses while maintaining anonymity. The digital landscape is ripe with potential for faceless marketing strategies that allow for impactful partnerships without the need for personal branding. By leveraging tools and platforms that prioritize collaboration over visibility, individuals can maximize their reach and effectiveness while staying behind the scenes. This approach not only safeguards personal privacy but also enables a focus on content creation and strategic marketing efforts that resonate with target audiences.

One of the most effective methods of collaboration in this context is through anonymous influencer campaigns. These campaigns can harness the power of influencers who operate under a veil of anonymity, utilizing their platforms to promote products or services without revealing their identities. This strategy can create an air of mystery and intrigue, drawing in audiences who are curious about the messages being delivered. By choosing the right influencers and crafting compelling narratives, businesses can achieve significant engagement and conversion rates while maintaining a faceless presence.

AI-driven content creation tools are another vital component for those collaborating without visibility. These tools can generate high-quality content tailored to specific audiences, allowing creators to focus on strategy rather than the nitty-gritty of content production. By employing AI technologies, individuals can ensure that their messaging remains consistent and relevant, even without being personally involved in every aspect of content generation. This automation allows for a streamlined workflow that enhances efficiency and effectiveness in reaching broader audiences.

Voiceover marketing techniques present yet another avenue for faceless collaboration. By utilizing professional voiceover artists, businesses can create compelling audio content that communicates brand values and messages without the need for visual presence. This method not only enhances the emotional appeal of the content but also maintains the anonymity of the creators involved. Additionally, voiceover marketing can be seamlessly integrated into various formats, including podcasts, video ads, and social media snippets, maximizing the reach of the collaborative effort.

Lastly, privacy-focused ad strategies play a critical role in facilitating successful collaborations while ensuring that personal information remains protected. By employing data-driven customer persona development, businesses can create targeted campaigns that resonate with specific demographics without needing to showcase individual identities. This approach allows for the curation of user-generated content and the hosting of virtual events and webinars that engage audiences without revealing the personal details of the creators. Through strategic collaboration grounded in privacy and anonymity, individuals and creators can build influential online businesses that thrive in the digital age.

MEASURING SUCCESS IN ANONYMOUS CAMPAIGNS

Measuring success in anonymous campaigns requires a nuanced understanding of key performance indicators that align with the unique goals of faceless marketing. Traditional metrics such as brand visibility and direct engagement may not apply in the same way for those operating without a personal brand. Instead, focus on metrics that indicate the effectiveness of your content and the degree to which it resonates with your target audience. Metrics such as conversion rates, engagement on user-generated content, and the performance of AI-driven content can provide valuable insights into the effectiveness of your anonymous strategies.

Another critical aspect of measuring success is the analysis of customer feedback and behavior through data-driven customer persona development. By leveraging analytics tools, you can track how users interact with your content and identify trends that inform your strategies. This analysis should extend to monitoring the performance of virtual events and webinars, where you can gauge audience engagement through participation rates, questions asked, and post-event surveys. These insights not only help in refining your campaigns but also in understanding the preferences of your audience without requiring personal visibility.

Additionally, privacy-focused ad strategies present unique challenges and opportunities for measurement. As privacy regulations evolve, it becomes essential to develop metrics that reflect how well your ads perform while respecting user privacy. Utilize aggregated data to assess overall campaign performance without compromising individual user identities. This approach allows for a comprehensive understanding of ad effectiveness, enabling you to adjust your strategies in real-time for improved outcomes.

The utilization of automated social media management tools also plays a significant role in measuring success. These tools can provide analytics on content reach, engagement rates, and audience demographics. By tracking these metrics, you can ascertain which types of content resonate most effectively with your audience and adapt your strategies accordingly. Moreover, insights gained from stock footage and imagery utilization can inform your creative direction, ensuring that your content maintains a high standard while remaining faceless.

Ultimately, success in anonymous campaigns hinges on a systematic approach to performance measurement that prioritizes data and analytics over personal visibility. By focusing on conversion metrics, audience engagement, and the effectiveness of your content strategies, you can cultivate a thriving online business without the need for a personal brand. Embracing these measurement techniques will empower you to make informed decisions, optimize your campaigns, and achieve sustainable success in the dynamic landscape of faceless marketing.

CHAPTER 4: AI-DRIVEN CONTENT CREATION

Tools and Technologies for AI Content

In the realm of AI content creation, a variety of tools and technologies are available to facilitate the development of compelling material while remaining faceless. These resources allow creators to harness the power of artificial intelligence to generate, curate, and distribute content without the need for personal branding or visibility. From natural language processing platforms to advanced analytics tools, the landscape is rich with options that cater to the needs of those who wish to operate behind the scenes.

Natural language generation tools have become increasingly sophisticated, enabling users to produce high-quality written content with minimal input. Solutions like GPT-3 and other AI writing assistants can generate articles, social media posts, and marketing copy that resonate with target audiences. For individuals looking to maintain anonymity while still delivering valuable information, these tools can serve as essential assets in crafting messages that align with brand goals without revealing personal identities.

Voiceover marketing techniques have also evolved, with AI-driven voice synthesis technologies allowing for the creation of professional audio content. Tools that generate realistic voiceovers can be used for video presentations, podcasts, and automated customer service interactions. By utilizing these technologies, creators can enhance their content offerings while maintaining a faceless presence, ultimately expanding their reach and engagement without the constraints of personal visibility.

Automated social media management platforms are another key resource for those venturing into faceless marketing. These tools streamline the process of content scheduling, analytics tracking, and audience engagement, enabling creators to maintain an active online presence without the need for constant oversight. By leveraging AI algorithms that analyze user behavior and preferences, individuals can optimize their content strategies and ensure that their messages effectively reach their target demographic, all while staying behind the curtain.

Data-driven customer persona development is crucial for crafting effective marketing strategies, and AI technologies can significantly enhance this process. By analyzing vast amounts of data, these tools can uncover insights into consumer behaviors, preferences, and trends, allowing creators to tailor their content and campaigns accordingly. This approach not only improves the relevance of the material produced but also ensures that it resonates with audiences, maximizing the potential for engagement and conversion while allowing creators to maintain their anonymity in the marketplace.

CRAFTING ENGAGING CONTENT ANONYMOUSLY

Crafting engaging content anonymously requires a strategic approach that prioritizes quality over personal visibility. In a digital landscape where personal branding often dominates, individuals can still carve out a successful niche by focusing on the value of the content itself. This begins with a deep understanding of the target audience and their preferences. By leveraging data-driven insights, creators can develop personas that guide the content creation process, ensuring it resonates with intended viewers while maintaining the creator's anonymity.

Utilizing AI-driven content creation tools can significantly enhance the efficiency of producing high-quality material. These tools can generate articles, social media posts, and even video scripts that align with the brand's voice and objectives, all without revealing the identity of the creator. In combining AI with effective keyword research and trend analysis, content can be tailored to meet the demands of the audience, thus increasing engagement rates and driving traffic to various platforms. This approach not only saves time but also allows creators to focus on refining their strategies and exploring new content formats.

Voiceover marketing techniques present another avenue for anonymous engagement. By employing professional voiceover artists or utilizing text-to-speech software, creators can produce auditory content that captivates listeners while maintaining a faceless presence. Podcasts, narrated videos, and audio courses can build a loyal following and foster a community around the content. This method emphasizes the importance of quality audio production, as clear and engaging delivery can enhance the overall experience for the audience, creating a strong connection without the need for visual representation.

An effective strategy for faceless marketing is the use of virtual brand ambassadors. These entities, whether human or animated, can represent a brand's values and engage with the audience on various platforms. By creating compelling narratives around these ambassadors, businesses can foster a sense of relatability and trust, which is crucial in building a loyal customer base. Furthermore, automated social media management tools can streamline interactions, ensuring that the brand remains active and responsive without requiring the creator's direct involvement.

Finally, privacy-focused ad strategies are essential for maintaining anonymity while still reaching potential customers effectively. By utilizing targeted advertising methods that respect user privacy, creators can promote their content to specific demographics without compromising their identity. This approach can be complemented by curating user-generated content, which not only builds community but also provides social proof of the brand's value. By embracing these techniques, individuals can successfully navigate the challenges of faceless marketing, ultimately achieving online success without the need for personal visibility.

ETHICAL CONSIDERATIONS IN AI CONTENT

Ethical considerations in AI content are paramount for individuals and creators seeking to build successful online businesses while maintaining a faceless presence. As the landscape of digital marketing evolves, the reliance on AI-driven tools for content creation introduces a myriad of ethical dilemmas. One of the primary concerns revolves around authenticity and transparency. Consumers increasingly demand honest interactions, and the use of AI-generated content can blur the lines between genuine human engagement and automated responses. Ensuring that audiences are aware of the nature of the content they consume is vital in fostering trust and maintaining brand integrity.

Another significant ethical consideration is the potential for bias in AI algorithms. AI systems learn from existing data, which may carry inherent biases that can perpetuate stereotypes or exclude certain demographics. For those engaged in anonymous influencer campaigns or virtual brand ambassador roles, it is crucial to critically assess the data being utilized and the outputs being generated. Implementing rigorous checks to mitigate bias not only enhances the quality of the content but also aligns with the values of inclusivity and diversity that resonate with modern audiences.

Privacy concerns also play a critical role in the ethical landscape of AI content creation. As businesses leverage automated social media management and data-driven customer persona development, they must prioritize the privacy of their users. Transparent data collection practices and compliance with regulations such as GDPR are essential to maintaining customer trust. Creating content that respects user privacy not only adheres to legal standards but also builds a reputation for ethical marketing practices, which can differentiate a brand in a crowded marketplace.

The utilization of user-generated content raises additional ethical questions regarding ownership and credit. While curating content created by users can enhance engagement and authenticity, it is imperative to acknowledge and compensate the original creators. This practice not only respects intellectual property rights but also fosters a sense of community and loyalty among followers. Establishing clear guidelines for content usage and ensuring proper attribution can enhance the ethical standing of a faceless marketing strategy while reinforcing a positive brand image.

Lastly, ethical considerations extend to the use of AI in voiceover marketing techniques and virtual events. The automation of these processes can lead to efficiencies, but it is essential to ensure that the resulting content does not sacrifice quality for convenience. Engaging with audiences through thoughtfully crafted messages, even when utilizing AI tools, requires a commitment to maintaining a high standard of integrity. By balancing technological advancements with ethical practices, individuals and creators can build successful online businesses that not only thrive in the digital landscape but also contribute positively to the broader discourse surrounding AI and marketing.

CHAPTER 5: VOICEOVER MARKETING TECHNIQUES

The Power of Voice in Marketing

The power of voice in marketing is a compelling tool that can significantly enhance the effectiveness of faceless marketing strategies. In a landscape where personal branding often takes center stage, the ability to convey messages through voice can create a distinct identity for brands without requiring personal visibility. Voice serves as an emotional connector, allowing businesses to resonate with their target audience on a deeper level. By focusing on tone, inflection, and style, marketers can craft narratives that engage consumers and foster loyalty, all while remaining behind the scenes.

Voiceover marketing techniques have emerged as an essential component of this strategy. By utilizing professional voice talent, brands can maintain a consistent and polished auditory presence across various platforms. This approach not only elevates the quality of content but also ensures that messages are delivered in a manner that aligns with the brand's identity. Whether through promotional videos, podcasts, or social media ads, the right voice can amplify the intended message and create a memorable experience for the audience, encouraging them to take action without ever needing to know the identity of the creator.

Incorporating AI-driven content creation into voice marketing can further streamline and enhance the process. Advances in technology allow marketers to generate high-quality voiceovers quickly and efficiently, reducing time and costs associated with traditional recording methods. This automation enables individuals to focus on more strategic aspects of their marketing campaigns, such as audience engagement and content optimization. By leveraging AI-generated voices, brands can experiment with different styles and tones, tailoring their messaging to fit various customer personas and preferences, all while maintaining an anonymous presence.

Virtual brand ambassadors also play a crucial role in the power of voice in marketing. These digital personas can engage with audiences through voice, allowing brands to establish a relatable and trustworthy image without revealing the identities of the people behind them. This approach not only preserves privacy but also allows for creative storytelling that captivates audiences. By developing unique vocal personas, brands can create a strong presence across virtual events, webinars, and social media, fostering a connection with potential customers that feels both personal and authentic.

Finally, the integration of user-generated content curation into voice marketing strategies can amplify the brand's reach and credibility. Encouraging customers to share their experiences through audio testimonials can enrich the marketing narrative while providing social proof that resonates with prospective buyers. By highlighting real voices and stories, brands can leverage the power of community and authenticity, enhancing their appeal without sacrificing anonymity. In this way, voice becomes not just a marketing tool but a powerful catalyst for building trust and fostering engagement in the digital marketplace.

CREATING COMPELLING VOICEOVER CONTENT

Creating compelling voiceover content is a critical component in the landscape of faceless marketing, enabling creators to connect with audiences without revealing their identities. Voiceovers serve as a powerful storytelling tool that can evoke emotions, convey brand messages, and enhance the overall user experience. By mastering voiceover techniques, individuals can craft narratives that resonate deeply with their target audience, fostering engagement and loyalty while maintaining anonymity. This approach is particularly beneficial for those who prefer to operate behind the scenes yet wish to establish a strong online presence.

The first step in creating effective voiceover content is to understand the target audience and their preferences. Developing a data-driven customer persona can guide voiceover choices, including tone, pacing, and style. By analyzing user demographics and behavior, creators can tailor their scripts to meet the specific needs and expectations of their audience. This targeted approach not only ensures relevance but also increases the likelihood of capturing attention in a crowded digital marketplace. When the voice resonates with the audience, it creates an instant connection, encouraging viewers to engage further with the content.

Next, the script itself plays a vital role in delivering compelling voiceover content. A well-crafted script should be concise, engaging, and aligned with the brand's message. Incorporating storytelling elements can transform a mundane narrative into a captivating experience. Using techniques such as vivid imagery, relatable scenarios, and emotional appeals can enhance the script's effectiveness. It's essential to consider the rhythm and flow of the words, as this will impact the delivery and overall impact of the voiceover. A strong script not only captures attention but also motivates the audience to act, whether that means exploring more content, sharing, or making a purchase.

Once the script is in place, the choice of voice actor is equally important. The voice should reflect the brand's personality and values while appealing to the target demographic. Whether it's a warm, friendly tone or a professional, authoritative voice, the right choice can significantly influence how the message is perceived. Utilizing platforms that connect creators with professional voice actors can streamline this process, ensuring that the selected voice aligns perfectly with the envisioned brand narrative. Additionally, utilizing AI-driven tools for voice modulation and enhancement can further refine the audio quality, making the content more polished and appealing.

Finally, distribution and promotion are crucial for maximizing the impact of voiceover content. Integrating voiceovers into various formats, such as videos, podcasts, and webinars, allows for versatility in reaching audiences across multiple platforms. Employing privacy-focused ad strategies can help promote this content without compromising anonymity, ensuring that the brand remains invisible while still gaining visibility. Consistent analysis of engagement metrics will provide insights into what resonates most with the audience, allowing for continuous improvement in voiceover content creation. By leveraging these techniques, creators can harness the power of voiceovers to build successful online businesses without the need for a personal brand or direct visibility.

PLATFORMS FOR VOICEOVER DISTRIBUTION

In the evolving landscape of digital marketing, platforms for voiceover distribution serve as essential tools for individuals seeking to build successful online businesses while maintaining their anonymity. These platforms facilitate the seamless delivery of voiceover content to a broad audience without necessitating personal branding or visibility. Services such as Voices.com, Fiverr, and Upwork enable creators to showcase their skills and connect with clients without revealing their identities. By leveraging these platforms, voiceover artists can carve out a niche in the market, allowing them to focus on content creation and monetization rather than personal promotion.

The integration of AI-driven content creation tools has transformed how voiceover work is produced and distributed. Platforms like Descript and AIVA harness artificial intelligence to streamline the editing process, enabling creators to generate high-quality audio with minimal effort. This technology not only enhances the efficiency of voiceover production but also democratizes access to professional-grade tools, empowering more individuals to participate in the voiceover market without extensive training or resources. As a result, users can focus on crafting compelling narratives while the technology handles the technical complexities.

When considering voiceover marketing techniques, it is vital to explore how these platforms enable anonymous influencer campaigns. By collaborating with virtual brand ambassadors, businesses can leverage voiceover talent to amplify their message without compromising the privacy of the creators involved. This approach allows companies to maintain a consistent brand voice while also tapping into the growing demand for authentic and relatable content. As brands increasingly seek to connect with their audiences on a personal level, the role of voiceover artists as unseen influencers becomes ever more significant.

Automated social media management tools further enhance the distribution of voiceover content by providing creators with efficient ways to reach their target audience. Platforms like Hootsuite and Buffer allow users to schedule and manage their posts across multiple channels, ensuring that voiceover content is disseminated strategically and consistently. By utilizing these tools, individuals can maximize their reach without the need for constant engagement, allowing for a more hands-off approach. This is particularly advantageous for those who prefer to work behind the scenes, as it enables them to maintain a presence in the market while preserving their anonymity.

Lastly, the curation of user-generated content and the organization of virtual events and webinars provide additional avenues for voiceover distribution. By encouraging audiences to create content featuring their voiceovers or participating in online events, creators can foster community engagement and expand their reach organically. These methods not only enhance visibility but also contribute to building a loyal customer base that appreciates the value of the content being produced. In this way, platforms for voiceover distribution not only serve as a means of monetization but also as a crucial component in the strategy for achieving long-term success in faceless marketing.

CHAPTER 6: VIRTUAL BRAND AMBASSADORS

Defining the Role of a Virtual Brand Ambassador

Defining the role of a virtual brand ambassador is essential for individuals aiming to thrive in faceless marketing. Unlike traditional brand ambassadors who often rely on personal visibility and direct engagement with audiences, virtual brand ambassadors operate behind the scenes, leveraging online platforms to create and promote content without the need for personal identification. This anonymity allows them to harness various strategies that align with privacy-focused marketing efforts, enabling businesses to maintain a professional image while reaching targeted audiences effectively.

Virtual brand ambassadors serve as the voice of a brand, utilizing voiceover marketing techniques to convey messages that resonate with specific customer personas. This approach not only enhances brand identity but also ensures that the messaging remains consistent across multiple platforms. By employing AI-driven content creation tools, these ambassadors can generate engaging materials that appeal to diverse demographics without revealing their identities. This anonymity can create a sense of intrigue and curiosity among consumers, potentially increasing engagement and loyalty to the brand.

Furthermore, the role of a virtual brand ambassador extends to automated social media management. By scheduling posts, responding to inquiries, and curating user-generated content, they maintain an active online presence on behalf of the brand. This strategy allows businesses to engage with their audiences continuously while minimizing the need for constant personal involvement. The use of stock footage and imagery can complement this approach, providing high-quality visuals that enhance brand storytelling without the associated costs and time of traditional content creation.

In addition to promoting products and services, virtual brand ambassadors can effectively participate in virtual events and webinars. By representing a brand during online gatherings, they help create a professional atmosphere that attracts potential customers. This involvement not only strengthens the brand's credibility but also fosters community engagement. Through thoughtful interaction and the sharing of valuable insights, they can build trust with audiences, reinforcing the brand's commitment to quality and customer satisfaction.

Ultimately, defining the role of a virtual brand ambassador is about maximizing impact while maintaining anonymity. By employing data-driven strategies to understand customer personas, they can tailor their approaches to meet the evolving needs of the market. This strategic alignment allows businesses to navigate the complexities of faceless marketing successfully, ensuring that their messages are both effective and respectful of consumer privacy. As online businesses continue to grow, the significance of virtual brand ambassadors will only increase, making them indispensable assets in the digital marketing landscape.

SELECTING THE RIGHT AMBASSADORS

Selecting the right ambassadors is critical for individuals aiming to excel in faceless marketing strategies. The effectiveness of an ambassador hinges on their ability to resonate with the target audience while maintaining the anonymity that defines this marketing approach. Ambassadors should possess an understanding of the niche and the unique characteristics of the audience being targeted. They must embody the values of the brand without overshadowing it, allowing the products or services to shine through their endorsements. This alignment ensures that the message remains consistent and effective, reinforcing the brand identity in a subtle yet impactful manner.

When considering potential ambassadors, it is essential to evaluate their engagement metrics rather than their follower counts. High engagement rates indicate that the ambassador has established trust and credibility with their audience, which is paramount for any campaign. This trust is particularly important in faceless marketing, where the emphasis is on authenticity rather than personal branding. Ambassadors who can create genuine connections with their followers can effectively convey brand messages, leading to better conversion rates and increased brand loyalty.

Utilizing AI-driven tools can streamline the process of selecting the right ambassadors. These tools can analyze social media activity, audience demographics, and engagement patterns to identify individuals who align with the brand's values and target audience. By leveraging data-driven insights, businesses can make informed decisions about which ambassadors will best represent their brand, ensuring that the selection process is not only efficient but also effective. This analytical approach minimizes the risk of misalignment and maximizes the potential for successful partnerships.

Virtual brand ambassadors present a unique opportunity for anonymity in marketing campaigns. These digital personas can be programmed to embody specific traits and values that resonate with the intended audience, allowing for consistent messaging without the need for a visible individual. By creating avatars that reflect the brand's ethos, businesses can engage with consumers in a manner that feels personal and relatable, while maintaining the desired level of privacy. This strategy can enhance brand recognition and loyalty, as consumers often appreciate the innovative approach of using virtual representatives.

In conclusion, the process of selecting the right ambassadors requires a strategic blend of data analysis, audience understanding, and innovative approaches. As businesses venture into the realm of faceless marketing, they must prioritize authenticity and connection over visibility. By carefully choosing individuals or virtual entities that align with their brand values and resonate with their target audience, they can effectively leverage anonymity to build trust and drive engagement. The right ambassadors can transform the way brands communicate, enabling them to thrive in a digital landscape that increasingly values privacy and authenticity.

STRATEGIES FOR EFFECTIVE ENGAGEMENT

Effective engagement in faceless marketing requires a strategic approach that leverages the unique advantages of anonymity while still fostering meaningful connections with potential customers. One key strategy involves the utilization of AI-driven content creation tools. These technologies not only streamline the content production process but also enable creators to generate engaging materials tailored to specific audience segments. By analyzing consumer behavior and preferences, AI can assist in crafting messages that resonate deeply, thereby enhancing user engagement without the need for a visible personal brand.

Another important strategy revolves around the use of voiceover marketing techniques. This method allows creators to communicate effectively without appearing on camera, appealing to audiences through auditory experiences. By employing skilled voiceover artists or AI-generated voices, businesses can convey their brand message in a relatable manner. This approach not only maintains the anonymity of the creator but also builds a connection with the audience, as the human touch of voice can evoke emotions and foster trust, essential elements in driving customer loyalty.

Engagement can also be significantly boosted through the implementation of virtual brand ambassadors. These avatars or digital personas can represent a brand in a manner that is both engaging and relatable while remaining faceless. By utilizing advanced animation and AI technologies, brands can create characters that embody their values and mission. This strategy allows for innovative storytelling and interaction, providing a distinct identity that consumers can connect with, all while maintaining the anonymity of the actual creators behind the scenes.

Automated social media management is another vital strategy for effective engagement. By leveraging tools that schedule posts, interact with users, and analyze performance metrics, creators can maintain a consistent online presence without the need for constant visibility. This automation not only frees up time but also ensures that the content reaches the audience at optimal times, thereby increasing engagement rates. Furthermore, the data collected through these tools can inform future strategies, allowing creators to adjust their approach based on real-time feedback and analytics.

Lastly, privacy-focused ad strategies are essential in today's digital landscape, where consumers are increasingly concerned about their data security. Implementing targeted advertising that respects user privacy can enhance brand reputation and foster trust. By utilizing user-generated content curation, brands can showcase authentic experiences from their audience, creating a sense of community and encouraging further engagement. This approach not only minimizes the need for direct visibility but also empowers consumers to become advocates for the brand, enhancing organic reach and fostering a loyal customer base.

CHAPTER 7: AUTOMATED SOCIAL MEDIA MANAGEMENT

Tools for Automation

In the realm of faceless marketing, automation tools serve as essential resources for individuals and creators who prefer to operate behind the scenes. These tools streamline various aspects of online business management, enabling users to maximize efficiency while minimizing the need for direct visibility. By leveraging automation, creators can focus on producing high-quality content and developing innovative marketing strategies without the demands of constant engagement that often come with personal branding.

One of the most significant advantages of automation is the ability to manage social media platforms seamlessly. Automated social media management tools allow users to schedule posts, engage with audiences, and analyze performance metrics without the need for real-time interaction. This not only saves time but also ensures a consistent online presence, which is crucial for maintaining audience engagement. Additionally, these tools often come equipped with analytics features that provide insights into audience behavior, enabling data-driven adjustments to marketing strategies.

AI-driven content creation tools have revolutionized the way creators produce material. From generating articles and social media posts to creating visuals and videos, AI technologies can assist in crafting compelling content that resonates with target audiences. By utilizing these tools, individuals can maintain a steady flow of high-quality content while keeping their identities private. This approach also allows for the exploration of various niches without the constraints of personal brand visibility, making it easier to pivot and adapt to market trends.

Voiceover marketing techniques have gained traction as a powerful tool for faceless marketing. With an array of voiceover software and services available, creators can produce professional audio content for videos, podcasts, and ads without needing to appear on camera. This enables them to convey their message effectively while maintaining anonymity. Furthermore, virtual brand ambassadors can be programmed to represent a brand's voice and personality, providing an additional layer of engagement without requiring personal involvement.

Lastly, privacy-focused ad strategies are vital for those operating under a faceless marketing model. Automated tools that analyze customer personas and target ads based on user data help ensure that marketing efforts are both effective and respectful of user privacy. By employing user-generated content curation techniques, creators can enhance their marketing campaigns with authentic testimonials and reviews, further establishing credibility without revealing their personal identities. Together, these automation tools empower individuals and creators to build successful online businesses while remaining behind the curtain, capitalizing on the vast opportunities of the digital landscape.

CONTENT SCHEDULING BEST PRACTICES

Content scheduling serves as a vital component in the framework of faceless marketing, allowing creators to maintain a consistent online presence while minimizing the need for direct visibility. The first step in effective content scheduling is to establish a clear understanding of your target audience and their behaviors. Utilize analytics tools to identify peak engagement times across various platforms. By aligning your content release schedule with these insights, you can maximize visibility and engagement without the necessity of personal branding. This data-driven approach not only enhances reach but also reinforces your strategy as an anonymous influencer.

Next, implementing a content calendar is essential for maintaining organization and coherence in your marketing efforts. A well-structured calendar helps you plan content themes, types, and formats, ensuring a balanced mix that resonates with your audience. Consider incorporating diverse content forms such as stock footage, voiceover marketing techniques, and user-generated content curation. By planning in advance, you can also allocate time for adjustments based on performance metrics, ensuring that your content remains relevant and impactful throughout its life cycle.

Automating your content distribution through social media management tools can significantly enhance efficiency. These tools allow for pre-scheduling posts, which can save time and reduce the pressure of last-minute content creation. Moreover, they often come equipped with analytics features that enable you to track the performance of your posts in real-time. This allows for agile decision-making, ensuring that you can pivot your strategy based on audience engagement and preferences, all while maintaining your behind-the-scenes approach.

Another critical aspect of content scheduling is the integration of virtual events and webinars into your strategy. These events can be scheduled to coincide with relevant trends or seasons, providing an opportunity to engage your audience in a more interactive format. Even without a personal brand, you can create a compelling experience that positions you as a knowledgeable entity in your niche. Promote these events strategically across your platforms, utilizing privacy-focused ad strategies to target potential attendees while respecting their data preferences.

Finally, continuous evaluation and refinement of your scheduling strategy are paramount. Regularly analyze the performance data of your content to discern what resonates most with your audience. Adjust your scheduling frequency, timing, and content types based on these insights to enhance engagement. This iterative process not only improves your content strategy but also fosters a deeper understanding of your audience's evolving needs and preferences, solidifying your position in the faceless marketing landscape without the need for overt visibility.

ANALYZING ENGAGEMENT METRICS

Engagement metrics serve as critical indicators of how well an online business connects with its audience, especially for those who prefer to operate without a personal brand. By analyzing these metrics, individuals can gain insights into user behavior, preferences, and overall interaction with the content. Metrics such as likes, shares, comments, and click-through rates provide quantifiable data that can inform strategies to enhance engagement. In the context of faceless marketing, understanding these metrics allows creators to refine their approaches, ensuring that their content resonates with target audiences while maintaining anonymity.

One of the key metrics to analyze is the engagement rate, which reflects the level of interaction relative to the size of the audience. This metric is particularly valuable for anonymous influencer campaigns where the focus is on content quality rather than personal identity. A high engagement rate indicates that the content is compelling and effective, while a low rate may signal the need for a reassessment of the content strategy. By leveraging AI-driven content creation tools, marketers can tailor their offerings based on the preferences revealed through engagement metrics, creating a feedback loop that continually optimizes performance.

Another important aspect is the analysis of user-generated

content, which can serve as a powerful engagement tool. By curating and promoting content created by users, brands can foster a sense of community and belonging, even without a visible brand figure. Metrics related to user-generated content, such as contribution rates and engagement levels, can provide valuable insights into audience interests. This information can inform future campaigns, ensuring that the content remains relevant and engaging, thereby enhancing the overall effectiveness of faceless marketing strategies.

Monitoring the performance of virtual events and webinars can also yield significant insights into engagement levels. Metrics such as attendance rates, participant interactions, and post-event feedback are essential for understanding what resonates with the audience. By analyzing these metrics, creators can refine their future events to better serve their audience's interests and needs. Automated social media management tools can facilitate this analysis, providing real-time data that helps in adjusting strategies on the fly, ensuring that the content remains engaging and impactful.

Finally, privacy-focused ad strategies must also take engagement metrics into account. As privacy concerns grow, understanding how audience engagement is influenced by data usage and targeted advertising becomes crucial. By analyzing metrics related to ad performance and user reactions, businesses can navigate the delicate balance between effective marketing and user privacy. This analytical approach enables creators to build trust and maintain engagement without compromising their anonymity, ultimately leading to sustained success in the realm of faceless marketing.

CHAPTER 8: PRIVACY-FOCUSED AD STRATEGIES

Understanding Data Privacy Regulations

In the digital landscape, understanding data privacy regulations is essential for individuals and creators aiming to build successful online businesses while maintaining anonymity. The rise of online marketing has led to an increased focus on data protection laws that govern how businesses collect, store, and utilize consumer information. Familiarizing oneself with these regulations not only safeguards businesses but also enhances consumer trust, which is crucial for long-term success in faceless marketing. Key regulations such as the General Data Protection Regulation (GDPR) and the California Consumer Privacy Act (CCPA) set the groundwork for ethical data handling practices that all online entrepreneurs should adopt.

Navigating the complexities of data privacy can be daunting, particularly for those operating behind the scenes. However, grasping the fundamental principles of these regulations is vital. GDPR, for instance, emphasizes the importance of obtaining explicit consent from users before processing their personal data. This regulation applies to any business that targets consumers within the European Union, regardless of its location. Similarly, CCPA provides California residents with specific rights regarding their personal information, such as the right to know what data is being collected and the right to delete that data. Understanding these rights empowers creators to design marketing strategies that respect consumer privacy while still achieving their business objectives.

Implementing privacy-focused ad strategies is another critical aspect of aligning with data privacy regulations. As marketers, it is essential to shift from traditional targeted advertising methods that rely heavily on personal data to more privacy-conscious approaches. Utilizing anonymized data for audience segmentation allows businesses to refine their marketing efforts without infringing on individual privacy. Additionally, leveraging user-generated content can create authentic engagement while minimizing the need for extensive data collection. By fostering a culture of transparency and respect for consumer privacy, online businesses can cultivate a loyal customer base that feels valued and secure.

Faceless marketing can also benefit from employing automated social media management tools that prioritize data privacy. These tools can streamline content distribution while ensuring compliance with privacy regulations. By using automation, creators can maintain a consistent online presence without the need for constant manual input, allowing them to focus on content quality rather than quantity. However, it is essential to choose tools that prioritize data security and comply with relevant regulations, thus safeguarding both the business and its audience.

Lastly, understanding data privacy regulations enhances the effectiveness of virtual brand ambassadors and AI-driven content creation. These methodologies can thrive in a privacy-conscious environment if creators are diligent about how they collect and use data. For example, virtual events and webinars can be designed to collect only essential information while providing attendees with clear information about their data usage. By embracing a proactive approach to data privacy, individuals and creators can navigate the digital marketing landscape successfully, ensuring that their faceless businesses flourish while respecting the rights and privacy of their customers.

CRAFTING ADS WITHOUT COMPROMISING PRIVACY

In the realm of digital advertising, the challenge of crafting compelling ads without compromising privacy is paramount. As online businesses transition towards faceless marketing, it becomes essential to devise strategies that respect consumer privacy while still achieving effective engagement. The integration of privacy-focused ad strategies is not only a compliance necessity but also a means to build trust with your audience. By prioritizing privacy in ad campaigns, businesses can foster a loyal customer base that appreciates transparency and ethical marketing practices.

One effective approach to maintaining privacy is through user-generated content curation. By encouraging customers to share their experiences with products or services, businesses can create authentic advertisements that resonate with prospective buyers. This method eliminates the need to collect extensive personal data, as customers voluntarily provide their insights. Furthermore, leveraging user-generated content enhances brand credibility and allows for a more relatable marketing narrative. It shifts the focus from the brand itself to the community surrounding it, which is particularly appealing in a faceless marketing strategy.

Additionally, artificial intelligence-driven content creation tools can play a significant role in crafting ads that respect user privacy. These tools can analyze trends and preferences without needing to access sensitive personal information. By utilizing AI, businesses can generate relevant and engaging content that targets customer personas based on aggregated data rather than individual profiles. This approach not only preserves privacy but also enables marketers to deliver personalized experiences that feel tailored without invading personal spaces.

Voiceover marketing techniques offer another avenue for crafting ads while maintaining anonymity. By employing voice actors to convey messages, brands can communicate effectively without revealing the identities of the creators behind the campaigns. This method allows for the creation of engaging audio content that captures attention and drives engagement without compromising the privacy of the individuals involved. Voiceovers can add a personal touch to faceless marketing, making the content relatable while keeping the focus on the message rather than the messenger.

Finally, the utilization of automated social media management tools can streamline ad campaigns while ensuring that privacy remains a priority. These tools can help manage content distribution and audience engagement without requiring constant oversight or personal interaction. By automating these processes, businesses can maintain a consistent online presence while adhering to privacy guidelines. This not only frees up time for creators to focus on strategy and content quality but also reinforces the notion that successful marketing can be achieved without sacrificing the privacy of either the brand or its audience.

TARGETING WITHOUT BEING INVASIVE

In the realm of online marketing, the challenge lies in effectively reaching your target audience without compromising their sense of privacy or authenticity. The concept of targeting without being invasive is not only possible but essential for individuals and creators who aim to build successful online businesses while maintaining a faceless presence. This approach involves understanding the nuances of your audience's behavior and preferences, leveraging data and analytics to create tailored marketing strategies that resonate on a personal level without overtly intruding into their lives.

To achieve this, businesses can utilize AI-driven content creation tools that analyze audience demographics and engagement patterns. These technologies enable marketers to produce relevant content that speaks directly to the interests of their target market without the need for personal branding. By focusing on the preferences and behaviors of potential customers, businesses can craft messages that feel personalized and engaging, thus enhancing the effectiveness of their campaigns while preserving a level of anonymity.

Voiceover marketing techniques serve as another strategic avenue for faceless marketing. By employing skilled voice artists to narrate promotional content or product descriptions, businesses can develop a distinct brand voice without revealing the identity of the creator. This method allows for the delivery of compelling narratives that resonate with audiences while keeping the creator's personal brand separate from the marketing efforts. It cultivates a sense of intrigue and maintains consumer engagement through an immersive auditory experience.

Automated social media management tools facilitate the execution of campaigns that target specific demographics while respecting user privacy. By scheduling posts and analyzing engagement metrics, marketers can optimize their outreach strategies in real time. This automation not only streamlines the marketing process but also ensures that content is delivered at optimal times, enhancing visibility and interaction without the need for constant oversight or personal involvement from the creator.

Finally, privacy-focused ad strategies are paramount in today's digital landscape. By prioritizing user consent and transparency, businesses can build trust with their audience. Utilizing data-driven customer persona development helps in creating nuanced audience profiles that guide ad placement and content creation. This targeted approach fosters a sense of connection and relevance, allowing marketers to engage potential customers meaningfully while honoring their privacy. As the landscape of online business continues to evolve, adopting these methodologies will ensure that targeting remains effective without becoming invasive.

CHAPTER 9: STOCK FOOTAGE AND IMAGERY UTILIZATION

Finding Quality Stock Resources

Finding quality stock resources is essential for individuals and creators focused on faceless marketing strategies. In an environment where visual content plays a pivotal role in capturing audience attention, leveraging high-quality stock footage, images, and audio can significantly enhance the appeal of digital offerings. For those who prefer to operate behind the scenes, identifying reliable stock resource platforms is the first step in creating compelling visual narratives without the need for personal branding.

A diverse range of stock resource platforms is available, catering to various niches and requirements. Websites like Shutterstock, Adobe Stock, and Getty Images provide extensive libraries of professional-grade visuals and audio, suitable for any campaign. Additionally, platforms such as Unsplash and Pexels offer free high-resolution images ideal for businesses operating on a budget. It is crucial to evaluate the licensing agreements of these resources, ensuring compliance and understanding the terms of use to avoid potential legal issues down the line.

Beyond traditional stock imagery, the rise of user-generated content (UGC) has transformed the landscape of digital marketing. UGC can serve as authentic testimonials or relatable visuals that resonate with target audiences. Platforms like

Instagram and TikTok provide opportunities to source this content, but it is essential to establish clear permissions and attributions when utilizing someone else's work. This approach not only builds community engagement but also adds a layer of authenticity that can enhance marketing campaigns.

For those leaning into AI-driven content creation, several tools can help automate the sourcing of stock resources. AI algorithms can analyze trends and recommend stock images or videos that align with current consumer preferences. This data-driven approach not only saves time but also ensures that the selected resources are relevant and impactful. Incorporating AI into the process can streamline content creation, allowing creators to focus on strategic elements of their campaigns.

Finally, privacy-focused ad strategies highlight the importance of selecting stock resources that align with brand values and audience expectations. As digital consumers become more discerning about how their data is used, opting for stock resources that prioritize privacy and ethical considerations can enhance brand integrity. By choosing high-quality stock resources that resonate with the audience's values, individuals and creators can build trust and foster long-term engagement, ultimately leading to greater online success.

LICENSING AND LEGAL CONSIDERATIONS

Licensing and legal considerations are critical components for individuals and creators venturing into faceless marketing and online business. Understanding the legal framework surrounding content creation, brand representation, and advertising ensures that your strategies are not only effective but also compliant with relevant laws and regulations. As you navigate the digital landscape, it is essential to be aware of copyright laws, licensing agreements, and the implications of using third-party content, all of which can significantly impact your operational strategies and overall success.

When utilizing AI-driven content creation or stock footage, it is imperative to secure the appropriate licenses for any materials you intend to use. Copyright infringement can lead to significant legal repercussions, including fines and the potential removal of your content from platforms. Always verify that you have the right to use images, videos, or audio content, and consider opting for royalty-free resources or creating original content to mitigate risks. Additionally, understanding the licensing terms associated with user-generated content curation is crucial, as you may need explicit permission from creators to use their work in your campaigns.

Privacy-focused advertising strategies are another area where legal considerations come into play. With increasing scrutiny on data privacy, especially in light of regulations like GDPR and CCPA, businesses must prioritize compliance in their marketing approaches. If you engage in automated social media management or data-driven customer persona development, ensure that you are transparent about data collection practices and provide users with clear opt-in and opt-out options. This not only builds trust with your audience but also safeguards against potential legal challenges.

As virtual brand ambassadors and anonymous influencer campaigns gain traction, the need for clear contracts and agreements becomes paramount. Establishing terms of engagement with virtual representatives can protect both parties and clarify expectations regarding deliverables, payment structures, and content ownership. These agreements should also address issues like confidentiality and the use of personal data to prevent any breaches that could lead to legal complications. Taking the time to draft thorough contracts will provide a solid foundation for your collaborations.

Finally, it is essential to stay informed about evolving regulations and industry standards that may affect your marketing efforts. The digital landscape is constantly changing, and new laws can emerge that impact how businesses operate online. Regularly consult with legal professionals who specialize in digital marketing and intellectual property to ensure that your online business remains compliant and that you are aware of any potential risks. By proactively addressing licensing and legal considerations, you can focus on building and scaling your faceless marketing endeavors while minimizing exposure to legal liabilities.

ENHANCING YOUR BRAND WITH VISUALS

Visual elements play a pivotal role in enhancing your brand, especially for those operating in the faceless marketing space. Visuals establish an immediate connection with your audience, transcending the need for personal visibility while effectively communicating your brand's message. By strategically leveraging imagery, graphics, videos, and animations, you can create a distinctive identity that resonates with your target demographic. This identity not only captures attention but also fosters trust and recognition in a crowded online marketplace.

Incorporating high-quality visuals into your marketing strategy can significantly improve engagement rates across various platforms. For instance, AI-driven content creation tools can generate compelling visual content tailored to your audience's preferences. By analyzing user data, these tools can suggest imagery that aligns with current trends and resonates with your customer personas. This data-driven approach ensures that your visuals are not only eye-catching but also relevant, enhancing the chances of conversion without the need for personal branding.

Utilizing stock footage and imagery is another effective method to enhance your brand's visual presence. Stock libraries offer a wealth of professionally produced visuals that can be integrated into your campaigns. These resources allow you to maintain a consistent aesthetic while saving time and costs associated with original content creation. By curating a collection of visuals that reflect your brand's ethos, you can create a cohesive narrative that reinforces your message across different channels, from social media to virtual events.

Voiceover marketing techniques also play a crucial role in complementing your visual assets. Pairing engaging visuals with professional voiceovers can elevate the storytelling aspect of your content, making it more impactful and memorable. This approach allows you to convey complex ideas simply and effectively, enhancing audience retention and understanding. As a faceless marketer, this combination of visuals and audio can establish an emotional connection with your audience, increasing their likelihood of engaging with your brand.

Lastly, embracing user-generated content curation can further amplify your brand's visual strategy. Encouraging your audience to share their own experiences and visuals related to your brand not only fosters community but also provides authentic content that resonates with potential customers. This method not only reduces the pressure of constant content creation but also builds trust and relatability. By effectively managing and incorporating user-generated visuals into your marketing efforts, you can enhance your brand's presence and engagement without relying on personal visibility, allowing for a truly faceless approach to online success.

CHAPTER 10: USER-GENERATED CONTENT CURATION

Encouraging User Participation

User participation is a cornerstone of effective faceless marketing strategies. Encouraging users to engage with your brand, even when you operate behind the scenes, can significantly enhance your reach and credibility. By fostering a community where users feel valued and heard, you can create a dynamic ecosystem that fuels organic growth. This engagement can take many forms, from commenting on posts to sharing user-generated content, each serving to amplify your presence without requiring personal visibility.

To stimulate active user participation, it is essential to create an inviting environment. This can be achieved by utilizing platforms that encourage interaction, such as discussion forums or social media groups tailored to your niche. By posing thought-provoking questions or launching polls, you can invite users to express their opinions and experiences. This not only enhances engagement but also provides valuable insights into customer preferences and behaviors, which can inform your marketing strategies.

Incorporating user-generated content into your marketing approach can further incentivize participation. By showcasing content created by your audience, you not only validate their contributions but also create a sense of ownership among your users. This can be particularly effective when leveraging stock footage and imagery, allowing users to see their input reflected in your brand. Encouraging users to share their experiences or insights related to your products or services can lead to a rich repository of content that resonates with potential customers.

Virtual brand ambassadors can also play a pivotal role in encouraging user participation. By selecting individuals who resonate with your target audience, you can leverage their influence to foster a community atmosphere. These ambassadors can engage with users, share their experiences, and motivate others to participate. This strategy not only enhances visibility but also builds trust, as users are more likely to engage with brands that feel relatable and authentic, even if the creators prefer to remain behind the scenes.

Lastly, data-driven customer persona development is integral to understanding and enhancing user participation. By analyzing user interactions and preferences, you can tailor your engagement strategies to align with what resonates most with your audience. This approach allows for more personalized interactions, which can significantly boost participation. In an age where privacy is paramount, respecting user data while leveraging analytics can foster a deeper connection, ensuring that your community remains engaged and active in supporting your faceless marketing endeavors.

CURATING CONTENT EFFECTIVELY

Curating content effectively is a vital strategy for individuals seeking to build successful online businesses without the need for a personal brand or direct visibility. In the realm of faceless marketing, the ability to assemble and present content that resonates with target audiences can significantly enhance engagement and drive conversions. By utilizing various tools and platforms, entrepreneurs can aggregate valuable information, visuals, and resources that align with their marketing goals while maintaining anonymity. This approach not only saves time but also allows creators to focus on crafting a cohesive brand narrative that appeals to their audience's interests and preferences.

One of the most effective methods for content curation is leveraging user-generated content. This strategy not only fosters community engagement but also builds trust among potential customers. By showcasing authentic testimonials, reviews, and contributions from users, businesses can create a sense of inclusivity and relatability. This is especially advantageous for those operating behind the scenes, as it shifts the focus from individual personalities to the collective experiences and perspectives of the audience. Curating user-generated content can amplify brand visibility while reinforcing the notion that the brand values its customers' voices.

Incorporating AI-driven content creation tools can also streamline the curation process. These technologies can analyze vast amounts of data to identify trending topics, relevant keywords, and audience preferences. By harnessing AI, businesses can automate the discovery of content that resonates with their target demographic, ensuring that the curated material remains fresh and engaging. This not only enhances the quality of the content shared but also reduces the time spent on manual research and content assembly, allowing creators to allocate resources to other essential facets of their business.

Voiceover marketing techniques present another compelling avenue for effective content curation. By utilizing voiceovers in curated videos or presentations, businesses can add a layer of professionalism and engagement without revealing personal identities. This strategy blends seamlessly with various content formats, such as stock footage or imagery, allowing for visually appealing and informative presentations. Furthermore, voiceovers can convey brand messaging with clarity and personality, making the content more relatable and memorable for the audience.

Finally, implementing automated social media management tools can significantly enhance the efficiency of content curation efforts. These platforms enable businesses to schedule, post, and analyze content across multiple channels without the need for constant oversight. By automating routine tasks, creators can focus on refining their strategies and exploring new content avenues. In addition, privacy-focused ad strategies can complement curated content, ensuring that promotional efforts align with the values of the audience while maintaining anonymity. By embracing these tactics, entrepreneurs can cultivate a robust online presence that thrives on curated content, facilitating growth and success in the digital marketplace.

LEVERAGING UGC FOR BRAND GROWTH

User-generated content (UGC) has emerged as a powerful tool for brands aiming to expand their reach and foster authentic connections with their audience. By harnessing content created by customers or fans, businesses can cultivate a community that not only engages with their products but also actively promotes them. This organic form of marketing can significantly enhance brand visibility without the need for a personal presence, making it particularly appealing for individuals and creators who prefer to remain behind the scenes.

One of the primary advantages of UGC is its inherent authenticity. Consumers today are increasingly skeptical of traditional advertising; they seek genuine experiences and endorsements from real users rather than polished corporate messages. By showcasing UGC, brands can leverage the voice of satisfied customers to build trust and credibility. This approach resonates well with audiences, as they are more inclined to engage with content that feels relatable and trustworthy. For individuals and creators looking to succeed in faceless marketing, utilizing UGC can serve as a compelling strategy to foster brand loyalty and drive conversions.

Incorporating UGC into marketing strategies can also enhance customer engagement. When brands encourage their audience to share their experiences, they create a two-way dialogue that fosters community and connection. This not only allows brands to gather valuable insights into customer preferences but also gives consumers a sense of ownership and involvement in the brand narrative. For those utilizing automated social media management tools, integrating UGC can streamline content curation while maintaining an active and engaging online presence without requiring direct visibility.

The implementation of UGC can be further amplified through strategic campaigns, utilizing virtual brand ambassadors and anonymous influencer partnerships. By collaborating with individuals who resonate with the target audience, brands can tap into new customer bases while maintaining a low profile. These virtual ambassadors can create content that highlights the benefits of products or services, encouraging their followers to participate and share their experiences. This creates a ripple effect, as the shared content naturally expands the brand's reach and influence within niche markets.

Finally, analyzing UGC can provide critical data-driven insights into customer personas, enabling brands to refine their marketing strategies effectively. By understanding which content resonates most with their audience, businesses can tailor future campaigns to align with consumer preferences and behaviors. This iterative process not only enhances marketing effectiveness but also ensures that brands remain adaptable in an ever-evolving digital landscape. For those focused on privacy-conscious ad strategies, leveraging UGC allows brands to engage with their audience meaningfully while respecting their privacy, ultimately leading to sustainable brand growth.

CHAPTER 11:
VIRTUAL EVENTS
AND WEBINARS

Planning and Promoting Virtual Events

Planning and promoting virtual events requires a strategic approach, especially for those operating in faceless marketing. The first step is to define the objective of the event clearly. Whether the aim is to educate, entertain, or build a community around a specific niche, establishing a clear purpose will guide all subsequent decisions. Consider the audience's preferences and pain points; this insight will help tailor content that resonates with them. Utilizing data-driven customer persona development can illuminate the interests and behaviors of your target demographic, ensuring that the event's themes and topics are relevant and engaging.

Once the objective is established, the next phase involves selecting the appropriate virtual platform. Different platforms offer various features, such as breakout rooms, polls, and chat functionalities, which can enhance attendee engagement. Researching and choosing a platform that aligns with your event goals and audience preferences is crucial. Additionally, consider the technical aspects of hosting an event, from equipment to internet stability, as these factors can significantly impact the overall experience. A seamless technical setup helps maintain professionalism and keeps the audience focused on the content rather than potential distractions.

Promotion is an integral part of the virtual event planning process. Leveraging anonymity in marketing can be beneficial, using automated social media management tools to schedule posts and engage with potential attendees without needing direct visibility. Craft compelling messaging that emphasizes the value of the event, utilizing voiceover marketing techniques to create engaging promotional materials. Additionally, harness user-generated content curation by encouraging past attendees to share their experiences, which can serve as authentic endorsements for future events. This strategy not only builds excitement but also fosters a sense of community and belonging among participants.

To maximize attendance and engagement, consider implementing a multi-channel promotional strategy. This can include email marketing campaigns, targeted ads, and collaborations with virtual brand ambassadors who resonate with your audience. Privacy-focused ad strategies can help you reach potential attendees without compromising their data. Moreover, creating a countdown or teaser content leading up to the event can generate buzz and anticipation. Engaging with your audience through Q&A sessions or polls prior to the event can also enhance their connection to the content and increase participation rates.

Finally, after the event concludes, it is vital to gather feedback and analyze the overall performance. This data can provide insights into what worked well and what areas need improvement for future events. Utilizing stock footage and imagery from the event can also be an effective way to create post-event content, further extending the event's reach and impact. By continuously refining your approach based on collected data, you can enhance your virtual event offerings, ensuring they remain valuable and relevant to your audience while solidifying your presence in the faceless marketing landscape.

ENGAGING AUDIENCES ANONYMOUSLY

Engaging audiences anonymously presents unique opportunities for individuals and creators who prefer to operate behind the scenes. This approach allows for the cultivation of a brand identity that is less tied to personal visibility while still resonating with target demographics. By employing strategies such as faceless marketing, businesses can create compelling narratives and experiences that engage customers without the need for a personal brand. The focus shifts from the individual to the message, enabling creators to harness the power of anonymity to build trust and loyalty among their audience.

One effective method for engaging audiences anonymously is through the use of AI-driven content creation. By leveraging advanced tools, creators can generate high-quality content tailored to specific audience preferences. This not only streamlines the content production process but also allows for the customization of marketing messages that resonate deeply with potential customers. Moreover, AI tools can analyze audience behaviors and preferences, providing insights that enhance the effectiveness of marketing campaigns while maintaining the anonymity of the creators behind the content.

Voiceover marketing techniques further bolster anonymous engagement, allowing creators to convey messages and emotions without revealing their identities. Utilizing professional voiceover artists or AI-generated voices can bring a unique touch to promotional materials, videos, and podcasts. This strategy capitalizes on the power of storytelling, as the audience connects with the content rather than the creator. By focusing on delivering value through informative and entertaining audio content, businesses can foster a sense of connection and engagement with their audience, even in the absence of a visible persona.

The rise of virtual brand ambassadors and automated social media management platforms has transformed how anonymous engagement is achieved. Virtual brand ambassadors can represent a company or product without a physical presence, operating through avatars or animated characters that embody the brand's values and messaging. This innovative approach allows for consistent interaction with audiences across multiple channels while preserving the anonymity of the creators. Additionally, automated social media management tools enable businesses to maintain a robust online presence, curating user-generated content and engaging with followers without constant oversight, thus reducing the need for direct visibility.

Lastly, privacy-focused ad strategies and data-driven customer persona development are crucial in furthering anonymous engagement. By prioritizing user privacy and employing targeted advertising based on comprehensive data analysis, businesses can reach their ideal customers more effectively. This approach not only respects audience privacy but also enhances engagement by delivering relevant content to the right people. Utilizing stock footage, imagery, and user-generated content curation can enrich marketing efforts, allowing anonymous creators to present diverse, relatable experiences that resonate with their audience while maintaining a faceless approach. Through these strategies, individuals and creators can thrive in the digital marketplace without compromising their desire for anonymity.

POST-EVENT ANALYSIS AND FOLLOW-UP

Post-event analysis and follow-up are crucial components of any successful marketing strategy, particularly for individuals and creators working in the realm of faceless marketing. In the context of anonymous influencer campaigns and virtual events, the insights gained from evaluating the effectiveness of your initiatives can provide invaluable information. A thorough analysis allows you to assess what worked well, identify areas for improvement, and refine your strategies for future campaigns. This process not only enhances your current efforts but also strengthens your overall approach to engagement and monetization.

The first step in post-event analysis is gathering data. For virtual events and webinars, this may involve analyzing attendance rates, participant engagement metrics, and feedback collected through surveys. For campaigns centered around AI-driven content creation or voiceover marketing techniques, metrics such as reach, engagement rates, and conversion statistics are essential. A comprehensive data collection process will ensure that you have a solid foundation for evaluating the effectiveness of your marketing efforts. By leveraging these insights, you can create a more robust understanding of your audience's preferences and behaviors.

Once the data is collected, the next phase involves interpreting the results. Look for patterns and trends that reveal how your target audience interacted with your content. For example, if user-generated content curation was a part of your strategy, examine which pieces resonated most with your audience. This analysis can help you pinpoint the kinds of content that drive engagement and conversions. If certain elements did not perform as expected, consider potential reasons for this outcome. Understanding the 'why' behind your metrics will empower you to make informed adjustments moving forward.

Following the analysis, it is essential to implement follow-up strategies that capitalize on your findings. For instance, if specific content formats proved successful, consider doubling down on those formats in future campaigns. Additionally, maintaining communication with your audience post-event can foster a sense of community and loyalty. Automated social media management tools can help you maintain a consistent presence without overwhelming your resources. Crafting personalized follow-up messages or offering exclusive content can enhance engagement and encourage repeat interactions, reinforcing the invisible influence of your brand.

Finally, integrating your post-event analysis into your larger marketing strategy is key to ongoing success. Continuous improvement should be a guiding principle in your approach. As you refine your data-driven customer persona development, ensure that each campaign builds on the lessons learned from previous efforts. This iterative process not only enhances your marketing effectiveness but also positions you as a thought leader in faceless marketing. By leveraging insights gained from post-event analysis, you can create a sustainable model for growth that thrives on the principles of privacy-focused ad strategies and virtual brand ambassadorship, ultimately leading to greater success in your online endeavors.

CHAPTER 12: DATA-DRIVEN CUSTOMER PERSONA DEVELOPMENT

Gathering and Analyzing Data

Gathering and analyzing data is a crucial step for individuals seeking to build successful online businesses in a faceless manner. Through effective data collection methods, such as surveys, analytics tools, and social media insights, entrepreneurs can gain valuable information about their target audience without revealing their identities. These insights allow for a deeper understanding of customer preferences, behaviors, and pain points, which can inform strategy and content creation. By focusing on data-driven techniques, creators who prefer to remain behind the scenes can craft marketing campaigns that resonate with their audience while maintaining their anonymity.

Once data is collected, the next step involves thorough analysis. Utilizing data analytics platforms and software, individuals can dissect the information to identify trends, patterns, and correlations that may not be immediately apparent. This analysis enables the identification of customer personas, which are essential for tailoring marketing efforts. By understanding who their audience is, faceless marketers can design campaigns that specifically address the needs and desires of potential customers, ensuring greater engagement and conversion rates. This process is particularly beneficial for those leveraging AI-driven content creation tools, as the insights gained can enhance the relevance and effectiveness of automated content.

In addition to audience insights, analyzing competitor performance is equally important. By monitoring the activities of other anonymous influencers and brands operating within the same niche, individuals can uncover successful strategies and areas for improvement. Tools that track social media engagement and website performance can provide benchmarks for what works and what doesn't, allowing creators to refine their approaches accordingly. Additionally, understanding competitors' user-generated content can inspire innovative ideas for curating and leveraging similar strategies to foster community engagement without compromising anonymity.

Privacy-focused advertising strategies also play a significant role in the data collection and analysis process. By understanding the legal and ethical considerations surrounding data usage, faceless marketers can implement campaigns that respect user privacy while still being effective. This includes utilizing anonymized data and opting for advertising platforms that prioritize user consent. Such practices not only build trust with the audience but also enhance the credibility of the marketing initiatives, leading to more sustainable online business growth.

Finally, the ongoing process of gathering and analyzing data should be viewed as a dynamic cycle rather than a one-time task. Continuous monitoring and adjustment based on new data will ensure that marketing strategies remain relevant and effective over time. Virtual events and webinars can serve as valuable opportunities to collect real-time feedback, further refining customer personas and enhancing engagement strategies. As the digital landscape evolves, those who are adept at leveraging data will maintain a competitive edge, enabling them to thrive in the realm of faceless marketing.

CREATING ACCURATE CUSTOMER PERSONAS

Creating accurate customer personas is a foundational step in executing an effective faceless marketing strategy. Customer personas are detailed representations of your ideal customers based on data and research. For individuals building online businesses without a personal brand, developing these personas allows for targeted marketing efforts that resonate with the audience. By understanding the motivations, preferences, and behaviors of potential customers, marketers can craft messages and strategies that engage without revealing their identities.

To create accurate customer personas, start by gathering quantitative and qualitative data about your target audience. Utilize online surveys, social media analytics, and customer feedback to collect insights into demographics, purchasing behavior, and interests. This data-driven approach ensures that your personas are grounded in reality rather than assumptions. For instance, if you are targeting a specific niche, analyze existing content that resonates within that community. This insight can guide the development of personas that reflect the true nature of your audience.

Once you have collected the necessary data, segment your audience based on common characteristics and behaviors. Each segment can represent a different persona, allowing for tailored marketing strategies that align with their unique needs. Consider factors such as age, location, buying habits, and pain points. This segmentation process is crucial for faceless marketing, as it helps identify the most effective channels and messaging for each persona. A well-defined persona can guide your content creation, ensuring that every piece resonates with the intended audience.

Incorporating AI-driven tools can enhance the accuracy of your customer personas. These tools can analyze vast amounts of data to identify trends and patterns that may not be immediately visible. By leveraging AI, you can refine your personas over time, adapting to changes in customer behavior and preferences. This adaptability is essential in a rapidly evolving digital landscape, where consumer interests can shift unexpectedly. AI not only streamlines the persona development process but also helps maintain relevance in your marketing strategies.

Finally, validating your customer personas through real-world engagement is vital. Test your marketing messages and content with your target audience and gather feedback to assess effectiveness. This iterative process allows for continuous improvement, ensuring that your personas evolve alongside your audience. By actively engaging with your customer base, you can refine your understanding of their needs and preferences, leading to more successful faceless marketing campaigns. Ultimately, accurate customer personas empower creators to connect with their audience authentically, without the need for personal visibility.

TAILORING MARKETING STRATEGIES TO PERSONAS

Tailoring marketing strategies to personas is essential for individuals looking to establish successful online businesses without the need for a personal brand or direct visibility. Understanding the nuances of your target audience allows you to craft messages and campaigns that resonate deeply, leading to higher engagement and conversion rates. By focusing on customer personas, you can create a more structured approach that aligns with the preferences and behaviors of your ideal audience. This method not only streamlines your marketing efforts but also enhances the effectiveness of your campaigns.

To effectively tailor your marketing strategies, start by developing detailed customer personas based on data-driven insights. Use analytics tools to gather information about your audience's demographics, interests, pain points, and online behaviors. This data will help you segment your audience into specific personas, which can inform your content creation, advertising, and engagement strategies. For example, if your analysis reveals a significant portion of your audience prefers video content, you may choose to invest in stock footage and imagery, enhancing your marketing materials while maintaining a faceless presence.

In the realm of faceless marketing, employing anonymous

influencer campaigns can be particularly powerful. By collaborating with virtual brand ambassadors who align with your customer personas, you can leverage their influence while maintaining your anonymity. These partnerships can take various forms, from co-branded content to social media takeovers, all designed to appeal to the specific preferences of your target market. This approach not only helps you reach a broader audience but also builds credibility and trust through association with established influencers in your niche.

AI-driven content creation can further enhance the personalization of your marketing strategies. By utilizing AI tools, you can generate tailored content that speaks directly to the interests and needs of each customer persona. This level of customization increases the likelihood of engagement, as users feel that the content is specifically designed for them. Additionally, incorporating voiceover marketing techniques can add a personal touch to your faceless campaigns, allowing you to convey your brand message effectively while maintaining the desired level of anonymity.

Finally, privacy-focused ad strategies are becoming increasingly important in a digital landscape where consumers are more conscious about their data. By aligning your marketing strategies with the values of your target personas, you can build a loyal customer base that appreciates your commitment to their privacy. Incorporating user-generated content curation and hosting virtual events or webinars can further engage your audience, providing them with valuable experiences while reinforcing your brand's connection to their needs and preferences. In this way, tailoring your marketing strategies to personas not only enhances effectiveness but also fosters a deeper relationship with your audience.

CHAPTER 13: CONCLUSION: EMBRACING THE FACELESS FUTURE

The Evolution of Marketing

The evolution of marketing has undergone transformative changes shaped by technological advancements, consumer behavior, and the increasing importance of digital channels. In the early days, marketing relied heavily on direct visibility, with businesses promoting their products through traditional media such as print, radio, and television. However, the rise of the internet and social media platforms has created a paradigm shift, allowing for innovative strategies that prioritize faceless marketing. This shift enables individuals and creators to build successful online businesses without the need for personal branding, focusing instead on the effectiveness of their marketing tactics.

As marketing strategies evolved, the concept of anonymity gained traction, leading to the emergence of anonymous influencer campaigns. This approach allows brands to leverage the reach and engagement of influencers without requiring those influencers to reveal their identities. By utilizing virtual brand ambassadors, businesses can maintain a level of privacy while still connecting with their target audience. This method not only appeals to consumers who value authenticity but also caters to creators who prefer to operate behind the scenes, effectively positioning them as key players in the marketing landscape.

AI-driven content creation has revolutionized how businesses generate and distribute marketing materials. Automation tools enable the creation of high-quality content tailored to specific audiences, streamlining the production process and enhancing efficiency. This technology also supports voiceover marketing techniques, allowing creators to produce engaging audio content without needing to appear on camera. By harnessing these tools, individuals can cultivate a professional online presence while remaining anonymous, making it possible to engage with consumers in a meaningful way without sacrificing their privacy.

Automated social media management has emerged as a critical component of modern marketing strategies. These tools help businesses maintain a consistent online presence by scheduling posts, analyzing engagement metrics, and optimizing content for various platforms. Privacy-focused ad strategies further enhance this approach, allowing brands to target their audience effectively while respecting consumer data. By leveraging these technologies, individuals can build their online businesses and reach potential customers without drawing attention to themselves, allowing them to thrive in a competitive digital marketplace.

The use of user-generated content curation and virtual events has also become increasingly popular, providing opportunities for individuals to connect with their audience authentically. By encouraging customers to share their experiences and contributions, brands can foster a sense of community while showcasing their products in a relatable manner. Virtual events and webinars serve as platforms for engagement, enabling creators to share valuable insights and knowledge without the pressure of personal visibility. Together, these strategies illustrate the ongoing evolution of marketing, emphasizing the potential for success in the online space without the need for a prominent personal brand.

FINAL THOUGHTS ON BUILDING SUCCESS ANONYMOUSLY

Building success anonymously in the digital landscape offers unique advantages for those who prefer to operate behind the scenes. The rise of faceless marketing strategies allows individuals to cultivate profitable online businesses without the pressure of personal branding or public visibility. This approach empowers creators to harness their skills and talents in various niches, such as AI-driven content creation and voiceover marketing techniques, while maintaining their privacy. By leveraging these innovative methods, entrepreneurs can establish a strong online presence that resonates with their target audience without sacrificing their anonymity.

Central to this success is the concept of automated social media management, which streamlines the process of content distribution and engagement. By utilizing advanced tools and software, individuals can schedule posts, analyze performance metrics, and interact with followers without the need for constant oversight. This not only saves time but also allows creators to focus on producing high-quality content that aligns with their brand's message. Moreover, privacy-focused ad strategies ensure that marketing efforts are both effective and respectful of user data, enabling businesses to reach their audience while adhering to ethical standards.

The potential of virtual brand ambassadors cannot be overlooked in the context of anonymous marketing. These digital representatives can engage with audiences on behalf of a business, creating an authentic connection without revealing the creator's identity. Through carefully curated user-generated content and strategic collaborations, businesses can enhance their credibility and foster community engagement, which is critical for long-term success. This approach allows creators to build a loyal customer base while remaining comfortably behind the scenes.

Incorporating stock footage and imagery into marketing campaigns enhances visual storytelling, further supporting an anonymous approach. By utilizing high-quality, royalty-free assets, creators can convey their message effectively without the need for personal visuals. This strategy not only saves resources but also allows for a diverse range of content that can be tailored to specific audience preferences. As the demand for visually appealing content continues to grow, embracing this method becomes essential for those seeking to maintain anonymity while achieving impactful results.

Lastly, data-driven customer persona development is crucial for any online business aiming for success without visibility. Understanding the target audience's preferences, behaviors, and pain points enables creators to craft tailored content that resonates deeply with potential customers. By analyzing data and feedback, businesses can refine their strategies and enhance their offerings, ensuring that they remain relevant in a competitive market. In conclusion, adopting a faceless marketing approach opens doors to innovative possibilities, allowing individuals to thrive in their entrepreneurial journeys while maintaining the privacy they desire.

NEXT STEPS FOR ASPIRING FACELESS MARKETERS

To embark on a successful journey as a faceless marketer, individuals must first establish a clear understanding of their target audience. This involves conducting thorough research to develop detailed customer personas that encapsulate the demographics, preferences, and pain points of potential clients. By leveraging data analytics tools, aspiring marketers can gather insights that inform their content strategy and marketing efforts. Understanding the audience's needs will enable marketers to create resonant messaging that drives engagement and conversion without the need for personal visibility.

Next, aspiring faceless marketers should explore the various platforms that facilitate anonymous influence. This may include utilizing social media channels where content can be shared under a brand name rather than an individual's identity. Engaging in anonymous influencer campaigns allows marketers to connect with audiences through curated content that aligns with their interests while maintaining a layer of privacy. Additionally, considering partnerships with virtual brand ambassadors can amplify reach and credibility, as these entities often have established trust within their communities.

AI-driven content creation is another critical avenue for faceless marketers. By harnessing AI technologies, marketers can produce high-quality content efficiently and without the necessity of personal branding. This includes generating blog posts, social media updates, and even video scripts that can be disseminated across various platforms. Voiceover marketing techniques also play a significant role here, allowing marketers to produce audio content that resonates with listeners while remaining behind the scenes. The ability to automate these processes not only saves time but also enhances consistency and quality across all marketing efforts.

Automated social media management tools are essential for maintaining an active online presence without direct involvement. These tools enable marketers to schedule posts, engage with followers, and analyze performance metrics seamlessly. By employing privacy-focused ad strategies, faceless marketers can run targeted campaigns that respect user privacy while effectively reaching desired audiences. This approach ensures that marketing efforts are not intrusive, thereby fostering a more positive relationship with potential customers.

Finally, aspiring faceless marketers should consider the power of user-generated content curation. Encouraging customers to share their experiences and feedback can provide authentic content that resonates with new audiences. Moreover, hosting virtual events and webinars can establish authority and foster community engagement without the need for personal visibility. By strategically integrating these elements into their marketing plan, individuals can build a successful online business that thrives on the principles of faceless marketing, ultimately achieving their goals while maintaining anonymity.

DISCLAIMER

This book provides insights and strategies for faceless online marketing. While every effort has been made to provide valuable information, the effectiveness of these strategies may vary based on individual circumstances and market conditions. Readers should apply these ideas considering their specific needs.

PASSIVE INCOME HACKS

Unlock the secrets to financial freedom with Passive Income Hacks, an Amazon book series that guides you step-by-step toward building streams of income that work for you—day and night. Whether you're seeking to diversify your finances or completely replace your 9-to-5, this series provides the strategies, tools, and insights to make it happen. From mastering online business models like affiliate marketing and e-commerce to investing in real estate and stocks, each book reveals proven methods to generate wealth with minimal ongoing effort.

Perfect for beginners and seasoned entrepreneurs alike, Passive Income Hacks is packed with practical advice, actionable tips, and success stories from those who have achieved financial independence. You'll learn how to set up systems that generate income while you focus on other passions, giving you the freedom to live life on your own terms.

Affiliate Alchemy: Transforming Traffic Into Passive Income

Embark on a transformative journey into the world of affiliate marketing with "Affiliate Alchemy: Transforming Traffic into Passive Income." This guide demystifies the process of converting website traffic into a steady flow of income through proven affiliate marketing strategies. Designed for aspiring digital entrepreneurs, this book provides the tools and insights needed to create sustainable passive income streams online

"Affiliate Alchemy" offers a strategic approach to affiliate marketing, empowering readers to transform ordinary traffic into extraordinary income. The book dives deep into the core mechanics of affiliate marketing, including selecting the right products, optimizing traffic, and maximizing conversion rates. It provides actionable advice on leveraging search engine optimization, social media, and content marketing to enhance affiliate efforts. This guide not only teaches you how to set up and scale an affiliate business but also delves into advanced tactics for long-term success, such as building a personal brand and automating marketing processes to generate income while you sleep.

www.ingramcontent.com/pod-product-compliance
Lightning Source LLC
LaVergne TN
LVHW051536050326
832903LV00033B/4278